"My Most Embarrassing Moment"

A PHABulous chance to find out the embarrassing moments of the famous!

From bank robbers to Royalty – everyone's experienced an occasion that they wish had been different.

An hysterical collection of goofs and gaffs!

PHAB (PHYSICALLY HANDICAPPED AND ABLE BODIED) is a registered charity. A donation will be made by Hodder & Stoughton for every copy of this book sold. For more information about PHAB, please write to:

Tavistock House North
Tavistock Square
London WC1H 9HX

"My Most Embarrassing Moment"

COMPILED BY COMPLETE EDITIONS

With a foreword by

ROLF HARRIS

Illustrated by Ann Johns

KNIGHT BOOKS
Hodder and Stoughton

First published in Great Britain in 1989 by Knight Books

British Library C.I.P.

My most embarrassing moment.
1. Embarrassment
I. Johns, Ann
152.4

ISBN 0-340-51618-6

Printed and bound in Great Britain for Hodder and Stoughton Children's Books, a division of Hodder and Stoughton Ltd, Mill Road, Dunton Green, Sevenoaks, Kent. TN13 2YA (Editorial Office: 47 Bedford Square, London WC1B 3DP) by Cox and Wyman Ltd, Reading, Berks. Photoset by Rowland Phototypesetting Ltd, Bury St Edmunds, Suffolk.

Foreword by Rolf Harris

As President of PHAB, it gives me great pleasure to write an introduction to MY MOST EMBARRASSING MOMENT.

What a multitude of moments those four words conjure up. Some of them are caused by the sheer cussedness of events. Take this one for example: I was a painfully thin eleven-year-old member of a swimming club in Western Australia and at the end of the club races each week, all able-bodied members who felt so inclined would help with lifting the eight-foot-long wooden turning boards out of the water and transporting them to the club rooms for storage.

In those far off days men wore full-length cotton racing bathers, always navy blue in colour, with straps going over the shoulders. It was considered manly to slide the shoulder straps off after the races so that the chest and back could get a healthy-looking sun tan.

The most admired girl in the club was a stunning nineteen-year-old lass, Audrey by name, and I can remember as if it were yesterday my embarrassment when I stepped in to help carry the heavy turning board and realised that my swimming costume was slowly obeying the laws of gravity. I had peeled the shoulder straps off earlier on and as I struggled manfully past this lady I was trying to impress, my swimming costume slid right down my skinny frame and finished up around my knees. I daren't drop my end of the board as that would have probably plunged us all into the water.

Hardly anybody seemed to notice my sudden nudity, but I did, and the lovely Audrey did . . . and laughed!

When I was fifteen, I was a member of a group of youngsters in Western Australia who were singled out for special coaching in Art. We had an exhibition which was opened by Sir James Mitchell, the Governor General of the State. Ever-aware of opportunities for advancement, my Mum had encouraged me to do a portrait of Sir James from a newspaper photograph. It was hanging there in the exhibition and as the great man moved around my mother pounced.

'That's my son's work', she said, 'but he'd dearly love to paint you from real life.'

Ever the gentleman, Sir James said, 'Have the boy contact my secretary and arrange a time.'

My mother returned glowing to her cringing offspring on the other side of the gallery with the good news. Of course now it was up to me to make the arrangements. I got on my bike later in the week and cycled down to the phone box and armed with two pennies confronted the unfamiliar machine.

The secretary, sounding highly superior, arranged the portrait sitting with the following statement which is burnt on my mind for ever:

'Sir James can fit you in this Saturday. He can give you an hour from ten to eleven.'

On the appointed day I arrived, well in advance, or so I thought, armed with paints, canvas and a fold-up easel, and killed time until about twenty to eleven. I can remember thinking, 'It will look good if

I'm a bit early,' as I rang the bell precisely at twenty to the hour.

I had kept the Governor General waiting for forty minutes. I thought the secretary had meant an hour, from ten to eleven, until ten to twelve. You can imagine my embarrassment when the very irritable Governor said to the fifteen-year-old schoolboy, 'Young man, you're going to have to learn to be more punctual!' I couldn't even find the voice to try and explain.

I could fill the whole book with stories of *my* embarrassments, but that's not the plan. Read on and enjoy the many and varied events described here and take with you the thanks of all the members of PHAB.

And I know that PHAB members would also like to say thank you to the busy celebrities who have contributed their own embarrassing moments to this book. Thank you!

Rolf Harris

P.S. I painted the portrait of Sir James and it now hangs in the art gallery in Northam, Western Australia, the Governor General's home town!

TERRIBLY SORRY

Newspapers sometimes get things wrong and embarrass people. Take, for example, this announcement spotted in the *Ely Standard*. 'We apologise for the error in last week's paper in which we stated that Mr Simon Brown was a defective in the police force. This was a spelling error. We meant, of course, that Mr Brown is a detective in the police farce, and are sorry for any embarrassment caused.'

MUM'S THE WORD

You'll probably know GORDEN KAYE better as René – because he plays hapless bar owner René Artois in the BBC's comedy show *'Allo 'Allo*. In the programme René is always getting into terrible scrapes; and in real life, so does Gorden! 'Several years ago I used to leave my laundry with a service laundrette to pick up on my way home. A staff change brought a lady called Beryl, who was hopeless. She lost socks, made white shirts pink, damaged underwear, the lot. One day I called in and there was a new lady there.

"Where's Beryl?" I asked.

"Oh, Beryl's gone and I'm glad," she replied.

"So am I," I said, "she was useless."

"No, I'm Glad – short for Gladys," she replied. "And Beryl's my daughter!"' *Whoops* . . .

ON YOUR KNEES

A number of visitors to the House of Commons had an embarrassing time in 1979. They were being shown around by their MP, Neil Marten, and were impressed by the splendour and the atmosphere of the place. As they crossed the lobby Lord Hailsham, a very senior politician, recognised Mr Marten and called out, 'Neil!' And the visitors did, all of them falling to their knees in respect. Bet their faces were red when they realised what a mistake they'd made!

DOWN BOY!

A Manchester couple went on holiday to Greece and put their Alsatian dog into kennels for a fortnight. When they got home the husband dropped his wife off and then went straight round to collect the dog. It seemed well after its two weeks away but for some reason it wouldn't stop barking in the car. And once it was home it developed some other strange habits, like chewing the kitchen chairlegs. They decided that this was probably because the poor animal had been so unhappy in the kennels.

Then, almost a week after they'd brought it home, they received an embarrassed phone call from the kennel owner. Another couple who had boarded their Alsatian there were complaining that their dog now wouldn't come to them when it was called.

What's more, it had started to chase the cat – something it had never done before. You guessed it; the owners had taken home the wrong pets!

STORM IN A COCOA CUP

Thousands of Italians must have had red faces, too, after going to their local supermarkets and asking for *Cacao Meraviglio,* which in English means 'Marvellous Cocoa'. They'd seen it advertised on television in a comedy programme called *Indietro Tutta,* which makes fun of events in the news and sends up other TV programmes. The writers of the show decided to take the mickey out of some terrible TV advertising by writing their own adverts, and so they invented a product called Marvellous Cocoa. The whole thing was supposed to be a big joke, but thousands of viewers failed to get the satirical message. They thought the 'Marvellous Cocoa' adverts were rather good and went racing off to the shops to buy some – only to find that it didn't exist. In fact so many of them tried to buy it that a number of companies decided that it would be a good idea to manufacture some real *Cacao Meraviglio,* and at the last count *four* were all trying to obtain the rights to the name.

POISONED WORDS

It's very embarrassing to say something clever or insulting and find it turned back on you – as Lady Astor discovered to her cost. Winston Churchill, who later became Prime Minister, once had a terrible argument with Nancy Astor, the first woman MP, about women's rights. She thought women should have the vote: he didn't. After a long time arguing, Lady Astor said, 'Winston, if I was your wife I'd put poison in your coffee.' Quick as a flash Churchill replied,

'And if you were my wife, I'd drink it.' There's nothing you can say after that, is there?

TELEVISION EXPOSURE

Daredevil ANNEKA RICE may not be presenting *Treasure Hunt* these days, but her most embarrassing moment happened in front of millions of viewers as she raced around the country in search of hidden clues. 'My most embarrassing moment happened when I was filming *Treasure Hunt* in Somerset. I bent down to help a farmer load some hedge clippings into his truck and split my jump-suit right across the bottom. I spent the remaining clues running around holding a map to cover my embarrassment! People still write to me about this!'

HANDS UP

In August 1984 police were called to a house where a gunman had taken refuge and was firing at people in the streets. For two hours the police besieged the place, firing tear gas in at the windows and yelling to the gunman to come out and give himself up. Eventually an observer pointed out to them that the gunman had somehow escaped from the house and was standing just behind the police marksmen, begging himself to come out and give himself up. The police were, naturally enough, rather embarrassed.

THE HELPING HAND

A friend of mine has an elderly aunt who still blushes when she thinks of something she did as a little girl. She was out playing in the park with her mother one day when she noticed an elderly gentleman having trouble getting up from a park bench. After a few minutes she went up to him and held out a helping hand.

'That's very kind of you, my dear. My knees are so stiff,' he said. 'Are you sure you're strong enough?'

'Oh yes,' she said. 'I often help my grandad out of his chair when he's much more drunk than you.'

A SPLASH ON THE BACK

Fans of *Splash!* will know MICHAEL GROTH as one of the programme's presenters. But before he became a TV celebrity Michael was a pop musician – and it was then that he had one of his most embarrassing moments . . . 'I was in a rock band called Trickster, and we were touring Europe supporting the American band Boston. We were playing the big sports halls, holding up to 15,000 people.

'At one particular gig in Germany I had decided to wear the new pair of "moon boots" I'd just bought, complete with some leopard-skin tights (very nice!!). We were on stage and I was about to play a lead break; I moved towards the foot pedal, tripped up (the boots were very wide) – and ended up flat on my back. The lead break was played from this position, while I hoped no one would realise it was all an accident – fat chance of that!'

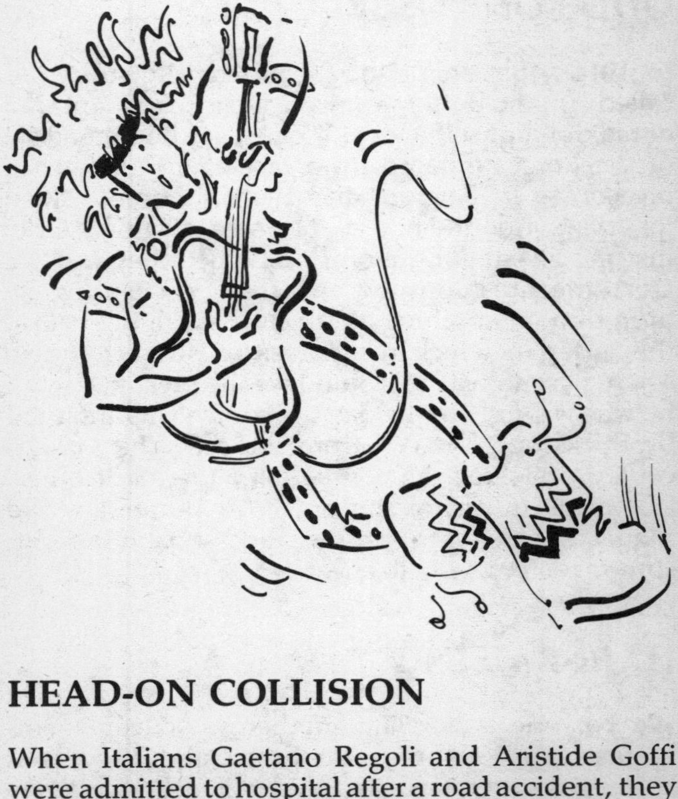

HEAD-ON COLLISION

When Italians Gaetano Regoli and Aristide Goffi were admitted to hospital after a road accident, they were very embarrassed about the silly circumstances of their crash. It happened on a narrow country road in thick fog. Both Gaetano and

Aristide had stuck their heads out of the window to get a better view. As they'd driven, unknowingly, towards each other they'd bashed their heads together so hard they needed hospital treatment!

ODDS-ON LOSER

In 1914 a British politician and racehorse owner called Horatio Bottomley dreamed up a brilliant way of making himself a lot of money. He bought all six of the horses entered for a race at a little-known racecourse in Belgium and then hired six British jockeys to ride the horses. He gave the riders strict instructions about the order in which they were to cross the finishing line and then, pretending he didn't know anything about this, laid a big bet on the order in which the horses finished the race. There was no way he could lose, he reckoned – but he was wrong. On the day the course was engulfed by thick fog blown in from the sea. The jockeys could barely see the course, let alone each other, and came in out of the order Mr Bottomley had requested. He lost a fortune – and serve him right, some say, for trying to cheat.

HAIR-RAISING!

We bet one Australian mother was deeply embarrassed in 1983 when the Prince and Princess of Wales were on tour Down Under. The Princess was on a walkabout in South Australia when she spotted a group of children and went over for a chat. One of the group was a young boy and she patted him on the head for a few moments before asking, 'Why aren't you at school today?'

'I was sent home,' he replied, 'because I've got head lice.' It is said that the Princess didn't bat an eyelid.

ALL WASHED UP!

Comedian JIMMY CRICKET found out at an early age how to make people laugh – though as he told us, it wasn't intentional. 'My most embarrassing moment was when I turned up late for school one morning. I walked into the classroom not realising that my trousers had shrunk in the wash. Needless to say it got screams from all the other kids, but I had to walk around all day with my trousers half-way up my legs.' So if you ever need to make someone laugh, now you know how!

MYSTERY TOUR

There was a report in a Sunday newspaper a few summers ago about a man and his wife who went to Great Yarmouth for their holiday. They were walking along the promenade one day when to their surprise they bumped into a number of people from the husband's firm. Apparently the company had organised a mystery coach trip and had brought the workers to Yarmouth for the day. The husband went off with his friends for a drink while the wife spent the afternoon on her own. When she went back to their bed and breakfast rooms she found that he wasn't there, and he didn't come home all night.

The next morning she called the police and reported him missing. They eventually tracked him down in bed at his home near Cambridge. Everyone had had such a good time in Yarmouth that they'd forgotten the chap was on holiday there with his wife. Instead of waving them goodbye, he'd got on the coach and gone home with them!

WRONG-WAY CORRIGAN

In 1938 pilot Douglas Corrigan took off from the airport at New York in thick fog. He was planning to head west, to California, but something went wrong and after 28 hours lost over the Atlantic ocean, he found himself flying over Ireland. He landed safely there and immediately told his Irish hosts that he'd flown the wrong way. This gave him instant fame as 'Wrong-way Corrigan', the man who didn't know east from west. At the time people were led to believe that it was just a crazy mistake, but research has shown that Corrigan had asked permission to fly his ricketty old plane over the Atlantic and had been refused because it was so old and unsafe. His 'wrong way' flight may just have been a way of getting round the regulations. Despite this, many people believed that his flight was an embarrassing mistake and the nick-name stuck.

LICENSED TO KILL?

Some years ago police in a Kent town received an hysterical phone call from a lady who said that she had seen a car driving past her house with two legs sticking out of the boot. Despite her shock she had remembered the vehicle's licence number and was able to describe it. A patrol car went after it and, sure enough, spotted two feet sticking out of the boot. Working with great caution, they flagged the car down and approached the driver, expecting to discover a crazy murderer. At that moment the feet sticking out of the boot began to wiggle and move, and a moment later a puzzled mechanic climbed out of the back of the car. It turned out that he was the driver's son who had been trying to trace the source of a rattling noise as his father drove along. Embarrassment – and a ticking off – all round.

TORTOISE TROUBLE

If you're one of the millions of viewers who watch *Blue Peter* twice a week, you'll know that MARK CURRY is the cheerful chap who tackles lots of amazing assignments. When we asked him about his most embarrassing moment he replied, 'On *Blue Peter* alone there have been so many embarrassing moments. The first was my very first programme as a BBC presenter. I was given a big build-up and an introduction second to none. I walked on – all smiles – and stood straight on the tortoise!! It's been downhill from there!!!'

GOING CUCKOO . . .

Until a few years ago the Washington Biological Survey was responsible for studying wildlife in the USA. Among the many wildlife projects master-minded by this organisation was one that studied the migration patterns of birds. Birds were caught and had a ring reading *Wash. Biol. Surv.* put around their legs. Then birdwatchers all over the country looked out for birds with these rings and told the WBS when they found one in their area. Everything was fine until one day the WBS received an angry letter from a farmer in Arkansas. He had shot one of the tagged birds as it had flown over his land and, seeing its leg ring, taken it home. 'My wife read the instructions on its leg,' he complained, 'and did as instructed; she *Wash*ed, *Biol*ed and *Surv*ed it. It was the worst thing I ever tasted in my life.' When he found out what had happened we bet he was embarrassed.

HAVING YOUR CAKE . . . AND EATING IT

This story has been told several times and in several different ways, so it may not be absolutely true. However, most of us have done something like it in our lives . . .

A lady went into a self-service cafe in a big department store and bought a cup of coffee and a KitKat chocolate wafer. She found herself a seat at a table, put her things down and went to get some sugar and a teaspoon. When she came back, the elderly couple sitting opposite her had opened the bar of KitKat, broken off half of it and were munching away.

As you can imagine, the woman was furious. What did they think they were doing, eating *her* snack? She reached across the table, grabbed the KitKat back and snapped a wafer off for herself. The couple looked at her very strangely but didn't say anything. After a few seconds the man picked up the last bit and ate it. The woman was so angry that she told the pair of them what she thought of them. They were nothing short of thieves, she said. And then she got up and stormed off.

Downstairs in the department store she saw a scarf she liked and opened her handbag to get her purse. There, lying at the top of her bag, just where she'd put it, was a KitKat . . .

DOG'S TALE

A young American man called Scott Brant was out late one night when a large, playful puppy came loping along the road towards him. Scott stroked it and it snuggled up to him, so he took it home and gave it some food. He'd never seen a dog quite like it before but it seemed affectionate. There was only one problem – it kept ripping up his furniture, and it was growing very quickly. Eventually he telephoned his local vet to see what advice he could offer. The vet took one look at the 'puppy' and immediately called the zoo. Scott was very embarrassed to admit that he hadn't been able to tell the difference between a puppy and a four-month-old lion cub that had recently escaped from the zoo.

PRINCELY PROBLEM

You may have seen JOHN SESSIONS being brilliantly funny on the TV show *Whose Line Is It Anyway?* – and if you haven't seen him you'll certainly have heard him because he supplies many of the voices for *Spitting Image*. He's also appeared in lots of plays on the stage, and it was while he was in a theatre that he had an embarrassing moment . . . 'Three years ago I was appearing in a play at the Lyric Theatre, Hammersmith. After the curtain call I ran downstairs in my 18th century costume and shot straight into Prince Andrew, who had come to see an old schoolmate in another play at the second theatre there. Without thinking I said, "What are you doing here?"

"Seeing a play," he said.

"Ours?" I enquired.

"No, the other one," he said.

"Well *that's* no good," I said. He laughed . . . luckily.'

'EAR, 'EAR

Bet Harold Senby, a Yorkshire pensioner, was embarrassed when he went along to a hospital in Leeds to have his hearing checked. Harold had been deaf for nearly twenty years and although he was fitted with a hearing-aid in his left ear it didn't seem to help much. When he went for his check-up the doctors discovered why; he was wearing the hearing-aid in the wrong ear!

OVER THE EDGE

After Kenneth Burke and Donna Kiehn were married they took their friends and relatives back to their sixth-floor flat in Philadelphia, USA. The friends wanted to take pictures of the newly-weds so Kenneth and Donna posed on the balcony.

'Back a bit,' instructed the photographers. 'Back a bit more.' Donna and Kenneth leaned hard against the balcony and then suddenly the rail gave way. Kenneth grabbed his bride to save himself and instead just succeeded in pulling her over the edge too. They fell seventy feet onto a patch of soft grass, and fortunately both were all right. But their friends with the cameras must have felt dreadful . . .

ALIAS SMITH OR JONES

Student Alan Smith was asked by magistrates to explain why he had given a false name to the policeman who had arrested him. A blushing Mr Smith told the court, 'I thought if I told them my name was Smith they wouldn't believe me, and I had no identification on me so I told them my name was Jones.'

SWANNING AROUND

Have you ever been to the opera? It's not just about fat ladies singing loudly, you know. Sometimes it's very funny. One time the audience got the giggles was in 1936 during a performance of *Lohengrin,* composed by Richard Wagner.

In the last act the singer in the starring role was supposed to be swept away across the stage by a boat steered by swans. Not real swans, of course; the whole thing was just made from wood and feathers and trundled across the stage on wheels. The swan-boat was supposed to roll a little way across the stage, stop so that he could get into it and then trundle off. On this occasion it stopped but, before he could get into it, took off again and disappeared. The singer stood there and watched it go. What an embarrassing moment! What was he going to do? How could the opera go on if he was stuck there in the middle of the stage? With a big sigh he turned to the audience and looked at his watch, as if he'd just missed a bus. Then he said very loudly, 'When does the next swan go?'

TIGHT SPOT

Actress JANE ASHER is a great supporter of PHAB. Her most embarrassing moment came at a party and is a lesson to everyone who gets undressed in a hurry!

'At a very smart party I felt something pulling behind me and preventing me from moving. I looked round and saw that someone was standing on a long, thick, black "string" which was trailing from the bottom of my black crepe evening trousers. I realised with horror that it was the tights that I had worn under the trousers on a previous occasion. When I had taken them off I had not bothered to separate them and now they were slowly exuding from the bottom of the trouser leg. I had to surreptitiously bend down and pull them right out. Very embarrassing!'

DON'T BANK ON IT

The *New York Times* tells the story of a bank robber who was so embarrassed by the assistant behind the counter that he chickened out of the robbery. He walked up to the counter of the Marine Midland Bank in Buffalo, New York, and told the bank clerk, 'I've got a gun. Hand over the money.'

He didn't know that this particular bank clerk had been held up several times before and was getting quite used to it. 'Show me the gun,' said the clerk wearily.

'I can't,' said the robber, 'otherwise everyone in the bank will see it.'

'Well give me a hold-up note,' said the clerk.

The robber didn't have a note, so he said to the clerk, 'Pass me a piece of paper.' While he was writing the note another clerk leaned over and asked the first what was going on.

'It's a hold-up,' said the long-suffering clerk.

'Oh, the hell with it,' exclaimed the robber and ran off.

THE FUTURE LOOKS BLANK

In 1978 there was a conference of clairvoyants held at a big hotel in Paris. Hundreds of palm-readers, fortune-tellers and astrologers turned up to discuss the future and as they emerged at the end of the conference a news reporter stopped one of them and asked, 'Is there going to be another conference next year?'

'I don't know,' said the clairvoyant, and then got very embarrassed. But not as embarrassed, we bet, as the person who ran classes teaching people how to see the future in a crystal ball. One afternoon his students arrived to find a notice on the classroom door reading, 'TODAY'S CLASS CANCELLED – DUE TO UNFORESEEN EVENTS.'

HASSLE FOR HARRY

HARRY SECOMBE, presenter of *Highway*, was once invited to sing at a concert held in Pentonville Prison. He accepted the invitation and everything seemed to go very well until he sang a song called *Bless This House*, a song for which he is famous. As he sang it he began to feel just a little bit embarrassed, for the words include the lines, 'Bless these walls so firm and stout, keeping want and trouble out . . .' Not the best song to sing in prison . . .

BATS IN THE BELFRY

Bell-ringers take their hobby extremely seriously and they sometimes attempt to set records for the number of peals and 'changes' they can ring without stopping. During one of these marathon bell-ringing sessions in a Buckinghamshire church, all the pulling and stretching caused one ringer's trousers to fall down. He was embarrassed and asked if they could stop while he pulled them up, but they refused – so he went on ringing, trouserless, for more than 5,000 more notes!

BAD DECISION

In 1962 a spokesman for the Decca record company listened to a selection of songs by an unknown group called The Beatles and said, 'We don't like their sound. Groups of guitars are on the way out.' For that reason, Decca turned down the chance to sign the most popular pop group the world has ever known. Bet that chap's still kicking himself!

BOTTOM LINE

LOUISE JAMESON is perhaps best-known for her role as Bergerac's girlfriend in the TV series *Bergerac*. Her most embarrassing moment was . . . 'being asked to lunch by a BBC producer to discuss a new series and being informed, an hour-and-a-half later, that my dress was tucked into my knickers – this after I had swanned around the bar doing my "hello darling" act to everyone . . .'

FIRE ALARM

When a house in Henley caught fire in 1973 and the owners called the Fire Brigade they unfortunately discovered that the local fire fighters were out on a special exercise and couldn't come to their rescue. *Fortunately* there was a fire engine available at Wallington, another town nearby; *unfortunately* it caught fire on the way and the firemen were unable to put the blaze out. *Fortunately* at that moment the Henley fire engine turned up. *Unfortunately* it didn't have enough water on board to put the Wallington fire engine fire out. By the time the Henley fire engine finally answered the emergency call to the house, the fire there had been put out by neighbours throwing buckets of water!

BABIES FOR FREE

In the early days of American films, cinemas used to try all kinds of publicity stunts to fool their customers into coming to see a film. One favourite was to announce in the local paper that to celebrate the opening of a new film, the cinema's owners would give a baby away. This, as you can imagine, provoked a howl of protest. Mothers and fathers wrote in from all around complaining that it was cruel and stirring up a great debate. The cinema owner would say that as the mother of the baby didn't mind it being given away, and as the baby itself didn't have any complaints, they didn't understand what was wrong.

More outrage and more letters to the newspaper followed, and on the day the cinema would be packed out with people waiting to see what happened. When they found that the owner was giving away a baby pig or dog, they were all very embarrassed at being so easily caught out.

SWEET NOTHINGS

A very embarrassed young lady drove her French boyfriend to hospital in Plymouth last year and told the doctors in the Casualty department that she had hit him over the head with a chair when she thought he'd insulted her. The poor chap had meant to say, 'Time stands still when I look at your face.' Sadly his English wasn't very good and what he actually came out with was, 'Your face, it can stop a clock.' His girlfriend had hit him before she realised that he was paying her a great compliment.

SURE BET

In 1988 a Scottish man stole £25,000 from the Post Office where he worked and used it to place four bets. He put £6,000 on Spurs winning the Cup, £6,000 on Scotland to beat Brazil, £4,000 on Bayern Munich winning the European Cup and the remaining money on a horse running in the Irish Oaks, intending to pay the Post Office back with his winnings. When he was arrested it was difficult to tell what he was most embarrassed about – the fact that he'd stolen the money in the first place, or that he'd lost every single one of his bets!

RUNNING COMMENTARY

Olympic medallist SEBASTIAN COE gets embarrassed by athletics commentators . . . 'In my running life, commentators' words have often caused me embarrassment. Not all the time of course – my mind, feet etc. are unaware of what's being said while I'm running. But later I see the faces, hear the chuckles and by the time I watch a replay I usually know there's a problem!

The one that most sticks in my mind is David Coleman's comment on the day of the Europa Cup, to the effect that, "The thing about Coe is that he can always get it up for the big occasion." Training at my club (Haringay) the following Sunday morning was not an experience to linger over. But all embarrassments have to be endured, don't they?'

HITTING THE WRONG NOTE

Comedian DICKIE HENDERSON once put his foot in it at a party where a woman with a terrible voice was 'entertaining' the guests with a song. He turned to the man standing next to him and commented on what a terrible voice the woman had. 'That's my wife,' said the man.

As you can imagine, Dickie Henderson was very embarrassed so he tried to make things better by saying, 'It's not really her fault, it's a dreadful song.'

This was the wrong thing to say, as he discovered when the man turned to him and said, 'I wrote it.'

CRIME DOESN'T PAY

A Canadian mugger must have been very embarrassed a few years ago when he attacked a man in the street and seized his wallet. Pulling $30 from it, he stuffed the money in his own wallet. Then before he ran off he threw the victim the empty wallet – except that it wasn't the empty wallet. When the shocked victim picked it up he discovered that the mugger had thrown him the one full of money and he was $300 better off than before!

THE CASE OF THE WRONG BRIDEGROOM

There was terrible embarrassment at a wedding in Ireland in the 1920s. The best man got muddled up and stood where the bridegroom should have stood. The priest didn't know the couple well and assumed that the best man, called Albert Muldoon, was the bridegroom. As he went through the service the real bridegroom was so nervous that he could barely say a word – so Albert said 'I do' and 'I will' for him. It wasn't until they went to sign the register after the service that they realised that the priest had married the wrong man! Fortunately there was time for another quick wedding, so they all went back to the altar and ran through the ceremony again – this time with Albert standing in the right spot and his mouth firmly shut.

AND THE WINNER IS . . .

For many years John Snagge was the voice of the Oxford and Cambridge Boat Race. His radio commentaries on the race were heard by millions, and so it was millions who heard one of his most embarrassing comments. During the last seconds of a particularly close race the two boats were absolutely even. As they neared the finishing line John Snagge said excitedly, 'I don't know who's ahead . . . but it's either Oxford or Cambridge.' Almost every year on Boat Race day his mistake is played back, so the embarrassment goes on . . . and on . . . and on!

ABEL TO HELP

British star athlete FATIMA WHITBREAD's most embarrassing sporting moment came when she was competing at an event in Portsmouth in 1987. 'I was competing for Great Britain against Czechoslovakia and I injured the lower area of my back. I needed to apply a pain-killing spray to the area but I couldn't do it without causing myself a tremendous amount of pain. My team colleague Julie Abel gave me a hand to apply the spray and in doing so she pulled my shorts down further than was advisable – with the result that the Sunday newspapers carried a picture of me headed "Fatty Bum Bum".'

THE TERRIBLE TOURIST

Poor Mr Nicholas Scotti. He made such an embarrassing mistake that people will still be laughing at him for years to come. It started in 1977 when he decided to fly from San Francisco, USA, where he lived, to visit his family in Italy. He got on the plane at San Francisco and when it touched down in New York to fill up with fuel he got off under the impression that he had arrived in Rome. He thought it was a bit strange that his family weren't there to meet him but he assumed they'd been held up in the traffic, so off he went to find their house.

As he wandered the streets in search of their address, he also thought it was strange that all the traditional Roman landmarks seemed to have disappeared. There was no Colosseum, no Forum, nothing. And even more odd was the fact that everyone seemed to speak English; even the street signs were written in English. Mr Scotti decided that this was because so many English-speaking tourists visited Italy. Eventually, speaking Italian, he asked a policeman the way to the bus station. As luck would have it the policeman was Italian and they had a chat, which made Mr Scotti feel even more certain that he was in Italy. But after traipsing around for twelve hours, unable to find his cousin's address, he was eventually handed over to another policeman. This one did not speak Italian, and it was not until Mr Scotti argued with him and said how surprised he was that the Rome police force employed policemen who didn't even speak Italian that it was pointed out to him that he was in New York. Mr Scotti refused to believe this. In desperation the police raced him back to the airport in a squad car, their sirens blaring. 'This just proves we're in Italy.' said Mr Scotti. 'This is how they drive over there.'

I SHOT AN ARROW IN THE AIR . . .

Do you ever watch old black and white films on TV? If you do, you'll probably have seen DOUGLAS FAIRBANKS, a wonderful actor who starred in many old swashbuckling movies. One of the most famous was his version of *Robin Hood* and to publicise the film he posed with a bow and arrow on a high roof in New York. The photographers urged him to actually fire the arrow and Fairbanks, without thinking too much about it, did. Well, he certainly got a lot of publicity from that incident, though it may not have been the kind he wanted. The arrow went whizzing towards the building opposite and landed up sticking in the bottom of a tailor who had been hard at work in his room there. The tailor raced into the street yelling about Red Indians and later took Fairbanks to court, where he had to pay $5,000 for the accident.

RUSSELL SEES STARS

Cuddly astrologer RUSSELL GRANT's powers of prediction don't always tell him what's coming . . . 'One of my most embarrassing moments occurred when I was walking along a crowded road, many years ago, deep in thought – and walked slap-bang into a lamp post! I did feel very foolish, and had a lovely black eye to show for it too!

'And there was another time when the zip of my trousers broke just seconds before being presented to the Queen Mum! Oh, blush!'

DOUBLED-UP WITH LAUGHING

Ever since he first appeared on stage, comedy star GARY WILMOT has been making his audience laugh – as he explained to us . . . 'On my very first appearance on stage I was just about getting started when the microphone slipped down the stand. Instead of stopping my act (or even just carrying on) and resetting the mike, I bent down to talk into it! Consequently my first stage appearance was performed with me bent double. I got lots of laughs and at the time I thought it was because my act was so funny – not because I looked so strange! I had a bad back for days after that!'

DAFT VADER

DAVE PROWSE is famous for his role as Darth Vader in the *Star Wars* films. He's also the Green Cross Code Man, which led to his most embarrassing moment . . . 'As Green Cross Code Man, I travel all over the world giving talks in schools to children in the 4–11 age group about child pedestrian road safety. My talk involves the children in a Question and Answer session and because I am known from the TV screen and also from the fact that I played Darth Vader in the 3 *Star Wars* movies, the children get very excited about my appearing at their schools. When I start the talks the children are all seated *en masse* in front of me, with the very young ones at the front and the older ones at the back. Most of my talk is geared towards questions and answers and although I want the kids to be enthusiastic, I still wish to be able to control them.

'At the outset of the talk I tell them, especially the young ones, that I do not want anybody shouting the answers out, I do not want anyone jumping up and down with their hands in the air, and that only the children who sit quietly will be chosen to answer the questions. (I might add that when I do the talks I am dressed in the Green Cross Code outfit, which makes me look a bit like Superman.)

'At that particular school I started my talk, but all the way through one little boy right in front kept jumping up and down, waving his hand in the air and shouting, "Sir, Sir!" – in short doing everything I had forbidden. Having already told them I didn't want this kind of behaviour, I ignored him for nearly the whole show. However, he was still getting excited, so I decided to show him up in front of the whole school for being naughty.

'I said to him, "At the beginning of this talk I told you not to jump up and down, shout out, wave your hands, and you just kept on doing it. What is your question?"

'"I haven't got a question," he replied, "but did you know, sir, your flies are undone?"!!!'

SORRY, MUM

When he was a teenager PRINCE CHARLES went to school for a while in Australia. One Sunday he surprised the local vicar by turning up for church. It was particularly embarrassing because there were very few other people there. 'I'm sorry there were so few parishioners,' he said after the service. 'It's a bank holiday, you see, and most of them have gone away for a few days.'

'Not another bank holiday!' exclaimed Prince Charles. 'What's this in aid of?'

The vicar went bright pink, then muttered, 'Over here we call it the Queen's birthday . . .'

RIPPON YARN

ANGELA RIPPON told us a very funny story about the time when she was an inexperienced reporter. 'I was sent to interview the new Earl of Mount Edgecumbe at his house in Cornwall. The door to the lovely Elizabethan manor house was opened by an elderly gentleman who asked my name, took my coat and showed me into the drawing-room. I naturally assumed he was the butler. After a few moments the Countess came in and rang for tea. It was delivered by the real butler, who was followed into the room by the "elderly gentleman" who turned out to be the Earl!! He was a New Zealander, with a real twinkle in his eye, who loved playing tricks on people. He was dubbed "the Reluctant Earl" by the locals, as he enjoyed being "just an ordinary bloke" rather than one of the aristocracy. I was to know him quite well after that, and realised that he would often answer the door to strangers without saying who he was. He said it told him a lot about people, when he saw how they behaved with someone they thought was a servant!'

PEOPLE IN HIGH PLACES

LADY ANTONIA FRASER once told the story of the time she and her husband went to a dinner party in terrible fog. One of the guests at dinner was a quiet, ordinary-looking little man on whom Lady Antonia took pity when she heard that he was stuck in London because the fog had caused his train to be cancelled. She invited him to stay the night at her house and he accepted. When she showed him up to his room she told him that the next morning, if he liked, he could have a lift into central London with her husband, who was at that time very high up in the government. 'You can have a ride in his nice big car,' she told him, feeling awfully sorry for him. 'That will be a nice treat for you, won't it?' He didn't say much and by the time she got up the next morning both he and her husband had already left for work. That evening when her husband came home she asked if the poor little man had enjoyed the ride to work.

'Yes,' said her husband, 'but I don't think it was much of a treat for him.' And then, to her terrible embarrassment, he explained that the 'poor little man' was in fact Sir William Armstrong, head of the civil service and a man who usually travelled in his own chauffeur-driven car!

AND NOW FOR NEXT WEEK'S NEWS . . .

Have you ever had the embarrassing experience of telling a white lie or making something up and then being found out? If so, you'll have some sympathy for Marion Crawford, who was famous in the 1930s and 40s for being governess to Princess Elizabeth (who is now the Queen) and her sister Princess Margaret. After her retirement in 1949 she wrote a book about her life with the Royal Family, which did not amuse them at all. But it was something else that caused her most embarrassing moment. She wrote regular features for a woman's magazine and in June 1955 one of her articles reported on the Trooping the Colour ceremony. 'The bearing and dignity of the Queen at the Trooping the Colour ceremony at Horse Guards Parade last week caused admiration among the spectators,' she wrote. She went on to describe Royal Ascot, saying that, 'it had an enthusiasm about it never seen before.' What's so embarrassing about that? you may ask. Well, both Trooping the Colour and Royal Ascot had been cancelled because of a rail strike! Crawfie, as she was known, had made it all up and there wasn't enough time to take it out of the magazine. As soon as it was published her secret was found out.

HELLO – AND GOODBYE

A well-known actress, who would prefer to remain anonymous, once held a party at her home. It was all going very well and she had enjoyed a few drinks with her friends, when three guests came towards her wearing their coats. She automatically assumed that they had put on their coats to go home. Actually, though, they had only just arrived. Swaying over to them, the actress got herself in a terrible muddle and heard herself say, 'Oh, must you really stay? Can't you go?' Now you know why she would prefer to remain anonymous.

WINDOW WIND-UP

NICK OWEN can be seen presenting all kinds of sports programmes, but his embarrassing moment is nothing to do with sport. As he told us, 'My problem is Do-It-Yourself work. I am always drilling holes in the wrong place and creating air bricks in our house where they weren't needed – and most of the shelves at home are at a slight angle, which wasn't intended. I always tell my wife Jill they add character to the place.

One day I had a problem with the car. The door handle had come off inside and in a fit of courage and inspiration I decided to have a go at repairing the damage. I was in the car for about half an hour in a state of increasing frustration and anger. I managed to take the inside door panel off and could see exactly what I needed to. However, there was a pane of glass in the way and hard as I tried to shift it, it just wouldn't move. I tried everything to shift it without breaking it so that I could get to the part of the door I needed to re-attach the handle. In desperation I went back inside the house to tell Jill that I was giving up.

"How stupid those manufacturers are to put a flaming pane of glass in such a ridiculous place!" I said. "And how on earth are you expected to get at anything the other side of it?"

"Have you thought of winding up the window?" she asked.

The awful truth dawned. I wound up the window; the pane of glass was no longer in the way and the job was done in seconds. I think it is fair to say that I am not a born handyman!'

FULL MARX

You've probably heard of the Marx Brothers, a group of zany comedians who made films in the 1930s and 40s and became famous the world over for their silly stunts. But the Marx Brothers didn't just reserve their tricks for movies. They were equally crazy in real life. One evening Groucho and Harpo Marx had been invited to an all-male dinner at a smart hotel. The person who was giving the dinner was getting married the next day and so the pair decided to give him a surprise. They had noticed that one of the lifts opened directly onto the dining-rooms on each floor, so they got in, pressed the button for the floor they were going to and then took off all their clothes. When the lift door opened again they leapt out – only to hear *female* screams and shrieks of shock. They'd pressed the wrong button and arrived on the floor where the bride and her female friends were having *their* party!

PIANO PROBLEM

Film-buffs will tell you that one of the best movies ever made was *Casablanca*, starring Humphrey Bogart and Ingrid Bergman. Even if you haven't seen the film you'll probably have heard the catch-phrase, 'Play it again, Sam,' which is addressed to the piano-player, Sam, who sings the lovely song 'As Time Goes By'. The character of Sam was played by actor and singer Dooley Wilson, and when *Casablanca* became a massive success he was booked by a number of nightclubs to sing there. It was all rather embarrassing for him, as it turned out when he arrived at the first nightclub and began to set up his microphone. 'Where's the piano?' asked the astonished nightclub owner.

Dooley Wilson had to explain that he can't play the piano. When they made *Casablanca* he just pretended to play – someone else actually recorded the music.

INSULTING BEHAVIOUR

A British politician was guest of honour at a dinner in New York earlier this century. He was due to make a speech after the meal so when coffee had been served and everyone was having a good natter the Mayor of New York turned to him and said, 'Shall we let the people enjoy themselves a little longer, or had we better have your speech now?' How very rude . . .

ROYAL GAFFE

A spectator at Hickstead, watching the show-jumping, turned to a young woman standing nearby and said to her, 'Has anyone ever told you that you look like Princess Anne?'

'I think I'm a bit better looking than she is,' said the woman – who *was* Princess Anne. How embarrassed the spectator must have been when he realised who he'd been speaking to.

CLOSE SHAVE

Like so many other people, *Give Us A Clue* star UNA STUBBS was embarrassed by an item of clothing. 'I once wore a silver skull-cap on *Give Us A Clue*. Close up it looked rather glamorous but in long-shot it looked as if my head was shaved!'

SKATING ON THIN ICE

The first roller skates were invented in the 1700s by Joseph Merlin. However, because of an embarrassing accident he had while wearing them, they did not become popular till nearly a century later. To publicise his new invention Merlin dressed up as a minstrel and wore his skates to a high-class fancy-dress ball. Everyone gasped as he came whizzing elegantly into the ballroom and proceeded to glide around the floor doing wonderful turns and spins, and all was going well when he lost his balance and went crashing into a priceless mirror. It shattered

into hundreds of pieces – and so did the expensive violin he had been playing at the time. Just a few minutes beforehand, everyone had wanted to buy some skates of their own. Now they all started to say how dangerous the things were. Embarrassed and injured, Mr Merlin left the ball. It wasn't for another hundred years that skates caught on.

LONELY HEARTS

There was embarrassment all round when a young man in America advertised in a Lonely Hearts column for a woman to go on a holiday to South America with him. He had one eager reply – from his mother!

THAT'S NOT CRICKET

This rather rude mistake was made by cricket commentator BRIAN JOHNSTON as he reported on a Test match between England and the West Indies. The batsman at the time was Peter Willey and he was facing West Indian fast-bowler Michael Holding. As Holding came running up to deliver the ball thousands of listeners heard Mr Johnston say, 'The bowler's Holding, the batsman's Willey . . .' *Whoops*.

TOMMY'S TROUBLE

You'll probably know TOMMY BOYD from TV-am's *Wide Awake Club*. He told us the story of his first star interview, with comic actor Brian Rix.

'It was my first "Big Name" interview: Brian Rix. It was fixed for me to visit him backstage at a theatre in Eastbourne. Come the time I was there, nervous, tape recorder in hand. There he was! I dived in: "How is the world's most celebrated *farceur* taking to the sea air?" I asked. He looked at me a bit funny.

'"Okay," he replied.

'"And how does it feel to make a living by dropping your trousers?"

'"Er . . ." he continued, "I wouldn't characterise it quite like that."

'I ploughed on. "Surely no-one really believes that in real life people make such dumb mistakes as you do on stage. Especially all those 'mistaken identity' jokes?"

'There was a long pause. "Are you under the

impression you are interviewing Brian Rix?'' he said. ''Because I'm Terence Alexander.'' (Now in *Bergerac*). Whoops!'

SHOW-OFF/SHOWDOWN

There's nothing more embarrassing than trying to be clever and then being taken down a peg. It happened to that great boxer Muhammed Ali once. He was travelling on a plane and the stewardess asked him to do up his seatbelt.

'Superman don't need no seatbelt,' said the cocky Ali.

'Superman don't need no plane, either,' snapped the stewardess. Muhammed Ali meekly did up his seatbelt.

Karen Allen, from Somerset, also got a bit big for her boots after she was voted the local beauty queen. One evening she was invited to attend a charity reception at the Town Hall to which a number of celebrities were coming. The Mayor, Mayoress and other important people were lined up, with Karen at the end of the queue. One of the celebrities, a well-known actor, arrived. He shook hands with the Mayor and Mayoress, members of the local council and everyone else. But when he got to Karen he took off his coat and handed it to her, apparently under the impression that she was the cloakroom attendant. Karen had been boasting to her friends all week about what she'd say to this famous visitor, but in the event she was so flummoxed she couldn't manage a single word.

TRANSLATION TROUBLE

There was embarrassment, not to say confusion, at an international conference when an English speaker used the phrase 'out of sight, out of mind'. The Russian delegates looked startled at this. No wonder. Their interpreter had translated it as 'invisible lunatic'.

RUDE LANGUAGE

You'll probably know comedian and quizmaster NICHOLAS PARSONS from his appearances on television. He was once asked to host a fashion show being put on to raise money for charity. All the models in the show were housewives and he had to interview each of them as they modelled their outfits. One lady revealed that she had been born in Germany, so Nicholas Parsons immediately launched into German-sounding gobbledy-gook – even though he barely speaks a word of German.

The lady he was interviewing went very pink in the face and told him off, in front of all the on-lookers, for saying such rude, insulting things to her. He ended up feeling just as embarrassed as she was!

WIRE-WOOL

It's difficult to imagine glamorous JOANNA LUMLEY ever looking anything but spectacular, but . . . 'I was shopping in a supermarket and carrying a wire basket which I had overloaded with heavy stuff. I got to the check-out and found that my coat button had got jammed through the wire and was held in place by heavy tins. I couldn't put the basket onto the counter and I couldn't pull free. In the end I had to take off my coat and leave it hanging onto the basket. Unfortunately under the coat I was wearing an incredibly holey jersey belonging to my son. Collapse of one "new Avenger"!'

NOW GET OUT OF THAT!

When a new prison complex was completed in Northern Ireland the designers felt so confident the place was escape-proof that they invited the SAS to come and try it out. Unfortunately the SAS men found all kinds of ways of escaping. They also found that some of the prison doors had been put in the wrong way round, so that 'prisoners' were allowed out but staff were kept locked in. Blushes all round!

HOLLYWOOD HOWLER

Hollywood film actress KATHARINE HEPBURN was embarrassed the first time she met the actor Spencer Tracy. Together they went on to become two of the most famous movie stars of all time, but when they first met Miss Hepburn didn't think much of Mr Tracy. 'I can see I'm a little tall for you, Mr Tracy' she said, trying to make him feel uncomfortable about his height. But it was she who felt uncomfortable when he replied instantly,

'Never mind, Miss Hepburn, I'll soon cut you down to size.'

SHOW HIM THE DOOR

Radio 1 disco jockey SIMON MAYO has a terrible tale to tell about an interview. 'My most embarrassing moment was when I finished an interview for my first full-time job in broadcasting at BBC Radio Nottingham. Instead of walking out of the door, I walked into the broom cupboard!'

THE GREAT ESCAPE

In a recent radio interview naturalist DAVID ATTENBOROUGH told the tale of an embarrassing moment that occurred years ago, in the early days of BBC television. Programmes were broadcast live from Alexandra Palace in north London. There were only two studios, so while a programme was going out in one of them, the other was prepared for the next show. David Attenborough was presenting a show about animals and one of the creatures he had live in the studio was a flying squirrel.

During the broadcast the squirrel managed to escape and when they looked for it later they couldn't find it anywhere. Everyone was rather puzzled, but the studios were busy and the programmes had to go on. It wasn't until three hours or so later that the squirrel turned up – in the middle of a religious programme. While a solemn gentleman talked about life, death and other serious matters, the squirrel climbed up the curtains behind him and sat looking into the camera. The poor chap had to keep going and the camera crew did their best not to laugh too much, while viewers at home watched avidly to see what the squirrel would do next!

SHOE SHUFFLE

Radio and television personality DEREK JAMESON sent us an extract from his book, *Touched by Angels*, in which he tells of his childhood in London and, in particular, his experiences as a wartime evacuee.

> 'At the age of 13, while a wartime evacuee in Hertfordshire, I entered an essay competition in support of one of those propaganda drives designed to stimulate fund-raising on the home front. This was on the work of the Red Cross, something normally that would not have inspired me to read the entry form. I got hold of some brochures on this worthy cause, read the lot and sat down to write my essay.
>
> My carefully researched words – first step in a lengthy career in journalism – carried off first prize in the Under-14 age group, much to the astonishment of the whole school and much of Bishop's Stortford. *What? A kid from that dreadful school! First prize. Whoever heard of such a thing.* I was pleased to learn the results had been read out

at Bishop's Stortford College, the local public school.

Collecting the prize was one of the blackest days of my life, a collision between the world I was to leave behind and my new role of earnest young thinker. It was ten guineas' (£10.50) worth of book tokens, a tidy sum in those days, to be handed over by the Bishop of Hertford at a posh Saturday afternoon fête in the Castle Gardens.

The problem was I had no shoes, only a pair of scuffed plimsolls. My teacher, Ernie Hare, gave me yet another note for the local Red Cross headquarters, where they doled out American welfare supplies. I feared the worst, having been there once too often in the past. Indeed, methinks I was their best customer. I should have explained the shoes were for an occasion to do with the good and kindly deeds of the Red Cross. Sadly, my tongue tends to freeze in the presence of do-gooders.

The lady read the note, sniffed and asked "What size?"

"Six."

"We haven't got anything in six."

"But I must have some shoes. Please, lady, it's very important."

"You're always in here," she said. "This is supposed to be for the war, you know, not the likes of you."

She gave me a look as if I were something the dog brought in, sniffed some more and went to the back of the shop. She returned with a pair of shoes all right. Size six. Bright yellow girls' shoes. With square toes.

"That's all we've got," she said, banging them on the counter.

God, let me die. What am I going to do? I took them away, trying not to show my despair. Back at the hostel, a ray of hope. Try to cover that bright yellow with black polish. I did it once, twice, half a dozen times. It just did not work. The black polish would not penetrate the yellow dye of the leather. I was left with a pair of shoes looking like someone had spewed over them.

They were marginally better than the worn out plimsolls. I had to wear them. Perhaps nobody would notice. It seemed like hours before my name was called over the Tannoy at the fête. I hurt so much inside that my body was shaking.

The lonely walk to the trestle table where the prizes were laid out seemed like ten miles. Every eye in the place must be on those square yellow shoes with black streaks. All those ladies and gentlemen in their summer finery.

The Bishop shook my hand, then gravely handed me the book tokens.

"Well done, Jameson," he said.

"Thank you, M'Lord," I replied in the way they had told me.

Then I noticed he was wearing gaiters. He looks like Pegleg Pete! And here am I dying a thousand deaths because some old cow at the Red Cross won't give me a pair of shoes.

I celebrated by spending the tokens on aircraft recognition books. Every last penny. They were required reading for lads of my age. Unfortunately the headmaster, Bertram Cartwright, did not always share our passion for the war effort. He congratulated me at assembly on Monday and told me to report to his study with my purchases.

"Aircraft recognition," he said when I got into his tiny study. He made it sound like a particularly evil crime. "What complete and utter rubbish! You disappoint me, boy."

Then he slowly dropped them one by one – there were five or six – into his wastepaper basket. He did not tear them up first, which I took to be an invitation to retrieve them when he was out of the way. I got them back in the dinner hour, much to the delight of my chums.'

(Reproduced by kind permission from TOUCHED BY ANGELS *by Derek Jameson, published by Ebury Press and Penguin Books.)*

PRESENT DISASTERS

Giving presents often leads to embarrassment. After all, how can you look pleased when your Great Aunt Mabel gives you *another* pair of woolly socks for your birthday? John Pilkington was embarrassed about the funny door-stop he bought his girlfriend Elaine last year. It was an old grenade, left over from the war, which John had bought from a junk shop. The person who sold it to him assured him that it had been defused and was perfectly safe, and John used it for several years in his own home. Then he decided it would make a good gift for Elaine. She left it in the porch of her home – which

was a good thing, because after a couple of weeks it blew up! John was, quite understandably, very embarrassed.

Another embarrassing incident involving presents happened to the late David Niven, the British film actor who appeared in many Hollywood movies. In Hollywood it was fashionable at Christmas for all the stars to give presents to everyone they worked with. Mr Niven duly bought Norma Shearer and Irving Thalberg, both very important people in the film world, six initialled handkerchiefs each. Can you guess what they bought him? A large car! Mr Niven's face was bright pink.

FLAMING DESIRE

Disc jockey PETE MURRAY once interviewed champion racing driver Nicki Lauda on a radio programme. Mr Lauda had been very badly burned in a terrible crash, so you can understand Pete Murray's embarrassment as he heard himself say, 'And do you have any other burning ambitions?'

SAFE KEEPING

It was reported in 1983 that Halesowen police had been called out to inspect a safe that had been dumped at the side of a road. A policeman stood guard over it until a crane arrived to winch it up and take it away. It wasn't until they'd been tugging helplessly at it for some minutes that someone noticed it *wasn't* a safe after all. It was an electricity junction box and it was cemented to the ground. The police were too embarrassed to comment on their mistake.

THE TRAIN NOW STANDING . . .

The Chairman of British Rail, Sir Peter Parker, had a deeply embarrassing moment in 1978. He'd been invited to attend a meeting in Cumbria and was driven to Crewe station to catch a train to take him there. Unfortunately his car was late and just as he ran onto the platform the train began to pull out. Waving his ticket, Sir Peter made a dash and leapt

on board – only to discover, after a few miles, that the train wasn't going to Cumbria but back to London, without stopping on the way! When he told the guard his problem, the guard wrote a message apologising for Sir Peter's delay and threw it out of the window as the train thundered through a station. Someone picked it up and phoned Cumbria to tell them their guest would be late. When the train finally pulled into London a red-faced Sir Peter jumped off it and began his journey to the north once more – though this time he didn't take any chances. He travelled by plane.

Another embarrassing moment said to have occurred on board a train involved a passenger who began to worry that he had left his kettle boiling away on the gas stove at home. The train was travelling non-stop to Edinburgh and he couldn't get off, so in a panic he asked the guard to help. The guard wrote a message requesting the police to break into the man's house and check the kettle, then wrapped it round a coin and threw it out of the window at a station. When the embarrassed passenger eventually arrived in Scotland he became even more embarrassed; the police had broken into his house and found the kettle on the gas cooker – but the gas wasn't lit!

And finally on the railway theme there's the embarrassingly wrong prediction of Dr Dionysys Lardner, who in the 1800s was professor of philosophy at London University. Told that newfangled steam trains would travel at more than forty miles an hour he said, 'Rail travel at high speed is not possible, because passengers would be unable to breathe.' Try telling that to the travellers on an Intercity 125!

KNICKER-LESS DAWSON

Funny man LES DAWSON also has an embarrassing memory involving a pantomime. 'I was playing the dame in pantomime in Leeds and in one scene I trotted on in my stage frock and did the "can-can" as an ad-lib. It got roars of laughter and I mentally decided to keep doing it for the run. Then when I got back to my dressing-room I found that I'd forgotten to put my underpants on . . .'

KEEP TAKING THE TABLETS

If you're a soap opera fan you'll know actor CHARLTON HESTON, who starred as Jason Colby in *The Colbys*. Before he became a TV star Mr Heston was a movie actor and one of his most famous roles was that of Moses in the story of the ten commandments. In one scene Mr Heston had to be shown walking down Mount Sinai carrying the two tablets of stone on which were chiselled the ten commandments. The props department wanted to make these of wood, figuring they'd be easier for Mr Heston to carry. However he insisted they be made of stone and so, at great expense, a stonemason made them. On the day the scene was to be filmed, Mr Heston went to pick them up – and despite being a very strong man, found he could barely walk while carrying them. What embarrassment! Fortunately it didn't take long before a pair of wooden tablets had been prepared and filming could go ahead.

MINCE PIES

Mrs A. Dixon wrote to a woman's magazine a couple of years ago to tell them about her most embarrassing moment. It happened one Christmas, when she was serving Christmas dinner to her parents-in-law. Mrs Dixon's mother-in-law was a very good cook and Mrs Dixon was rather nervous about getting everything right. However, Mrs Dixon isn't a bad cook herself and her freezer is always full of pies and casseroles and cakes that she makes herself. On Christmas day she opened the freezer door and took out some mince pies that she'd made a few weeks ago. She left them out to defrost and then popped them quickly in the oven while everyone had their turkey and Christmas pudding. 'Mince pies with your coffee?' she asked her guests.

'Yes, please,' said her mother-in-law, so Mrs

Dixon popped a hot pie on a plate and watched as her guest sprinkled it with sugar and poured cream over it. Slowly she took a spoonful – and instantly spat it out again. It was a mince pie all right – made with minced meat! Mrs Dixon had forgotten that she had made some little beef and onion pies to serve as snacks . . .

DOGGED BY TROUBLE

We wondered whether MICHAEL ASPEL might have an embarrassing tale to tell about one of the people he has interviewed on television – a famous film star or a politician, perhaps. And his story *was* about an interviewee, but not a human one . . . 'My most embarrassing moment was when I was interviewing a St Bernard dog and its owner for a television programme. The dog suddenly decided that I was its type and headed for me with the obvious intention of jumping on me! The most embarrassing part was that it was obviously in a very excited state and very passionate and I couldn't get it off. My honour was saved when four scene shifters pulled the dog off me!'

WHAT A SCREAM!

A newspaper in Hamburg, West Germany, reported the very embarrassing story of a housewife who was getting fed-up with her boring husband and her terribly boring life. They never did anything, they never went anywhere. One day, deciding that a terrible fright might liven things up, she hid in the wardrobe in their bedroom and, when her husband opened it, let out a blood-curdling scream. He was so terrified that he ran for his life, tripped over a chair and went tumbling through the open window. After that she had somewhere new to go each day for a month: the hospital – to visit him!

NAUGHTY VALENTINES

In 1985 a very embarrassing incident was reported in Manchester. It concerned Colin Rust, a young student who became very jealous when his girlfriend Hayley received three Valentine cards from boys in her sixth form at school. Colin was so angry that he went looking for each of the boys and told them to leave Hayley alone. He actually had a fight with one boy, during which he broke his rival's nose. The police were called and Colin found himself in court. The strange thing was that the boy Colin had hit swore he hadn't sent Hayley a Valentine card. Even stranger, the other two lads said the same. At last an embarrassed Hayley was forced to confess. She'd forged the message and signatures in the cards and sent them to herself to see if Colin got jealous. That way, she said, she'd know he really loved her!

THE REAL THING?

In the USA and Britain Pepsi-Cola was advertised with the slogan 'Come alive with Pepsi'. It proved very successful and sales of Pepsi boomed, so the advertising experts decided to translate it into Chinese and use the same phrase in Hong Kong and other Chinese speaking parts of the world. Unfortunately the Chinese translation caused a lot of embarrassment, for it turned out to mean, 'Pepsi can bring your ancestors back from the grave.' Understandably, all the people who'd bought Pepsi hoping to bring their ancestors back to life were very disappointed with the results.

UGLEY WOMEN ARE WONDERFUL!

The members of the Women's Institute in Ugley, Hertfordshire, got so embarrassed at being called the Ugley Women's Institute that they have changed their name to the Women's Institute (Ugley Division).

CORONATION ROBES

Coronation Street fans will know that actress THELMA BARLOW plays Mavis Riley in the 'Street'. Her most embarrassing memory is of a hot day one summer . . . 'I was picked up by a taxi and driven from Manchester to Blackburn on a day when the temperature was in the 90°s – remember those summers? I spent two hours opening a photographic studio, chatting to the public, posing for photographs, feeling that the effort I'd put into my make-up and clothes was all worthwhile. When I got home that night and hung my dress up, the back and "seat" were all covered in black creases – the heat and the dirty taxi seat had conspired against me. Thank goodness I was blissfully ignorant of it all afternoon!'

THE WORLD WILL END TODAY – OR MAYBE TOMORROW (OR PERHAPS NEXT WEEK)

In the USA in the last century a man called William Miller studied his Bible and came to the conclusion that the world would end on 3 April 1843. Hundreds of people took him seriously and began preparing for the End, when they believed everyone on earth would die. Some of them even killed their friends and relatives and then themselves, so that they could get to heaven before the end of the world. On 3 April, Miller and thousands of his followers climbed to the top of a hill and waited. Nothing happened, except when Miller tried to fly up to heaven using a pair of turkey wings – which, needless to say, didn't work. Was he embarrassed about getting it so terribly wrong? No, not a bit. He just announced that he'd made a slight error in his calculations and that the world would end on 7 July instead. On 7 July nothing happened – nor on 21 March 1844, nor on 22 October that year. After so long spent hanging around waiting for the world to end, Miller's followers began to feel a bit silly and, realising they had been fooled, drifted away.

AND FOR AN ENCORE

In the 1970s teacher Pat Hedger was a singer with a folk group. Most of the group's equipment was carried in a big trunk which, during concerts, was placed at the back of the stage. During instrumental numbers, when she was not needed, Pat would go to the back of the stage and sit on the trunk until it was time for her to sing again. One night she'd finished her song and walked a few steps back to the trunk. She didn't bother to turn round and check it but just sat down – and fell backwards into it, with her legs waving in the air for everyone to see. Someone had left the lid open . . . At the time it was very embarrassing but now she laughs at it. And, she says, despite her accident, it was one of the best concerts the band did.

THAT'S MY BABY?

A Los Angeles hospital had to admit an embarrassing mistake when they sent Mr George Schwenk a medical bill for $317. Mr Schwenk had gone into hospital to have an eye infection treated. The bill said that the fee was for 'delivering a baby'. Mr Schwenk wrote to the hospital saying, 'Please correct this error – or at least send me my baby.'

GYLES'S HEADACHE

If you watch TV-am or like reading, you're bound to know GYLES BRANDRETH. He not only appears on TV-am each week but he's written hundreds of children's books. He's also, from the sound of it, had hundreds of embarrassing moments . . . 'Embarrassing moments? How many of them do you need? They seem to happen to me each week, but one of my very worst occurred a few years ago at a party my wife and I went to. I didn't know many people there and I got talking to a terribly boring man who insisted on telling me everything about his new computer. Eventually I managed to get away from him to talk to a lady nearby. "I've just had the most dreadful chat with that chap over there," I said, half-jokingly. "He must be the world's biggest computer bore."

'The woman looked at him, then looked at me and said icily, "That man's my husband." As you can imagine, I was most embarrassed. Later that evening my wife and I were chatting to a man and I spotted the other couple sitting on the sofa. I said jokingly, "There's an amazing couple. He's the

most boring man in the world and *she* has absolutely no sense of humour."

'He looked at me strangely and then said quietly, "They're my parents." My wife insisted we go home before I could insult anyone else at the party!

'My most recent embarrassing moment happened only a few days ago. As you may know, I sometimes wear funny hats on TV and on this occasion I'd got a new one that looked as if it had a saw slicing through my head. I decided to wear it on TV and I made up some jokes about saws and having a headache and that kind of thing to perform while I was wearing it.

'Off I went to the studio, clutching the hat. Once there I had to wait around for a long time backstage before it was my turn in front of the cameras. Then suddenly they called me on without much warning and I dashed onto the set and began to do my little speech about having a headache this morning, and making lots of puns about sore/saw heads. They looked at me a bit strangely at first, so I kept pointing to my head and going on and on. Eventually someone began to laugh and soon everyone was having hysterics. Well, I thought to myself, it must have been even funnier than I'd planned. Then I put my hand up to my head – and realised I wasn't wearing the hat . . . Thank goodness the show wasn't going out live and we had time to tape it all over again!'

RED FACES ALL ROUND

Recent Oxfam statistics should perhaps make us all feel rather embarrassed. They show that just £1.50 a week is enough to keep someone alive on a subsistence diet. That's not embarrassing, you might think, until you put it alongside another statistic: in the UK the amount of money spent on alcohol each week averages out at £7 for each adult member of the population. That's right – the 'average' adult spends enough money on alcohol each week to keep someone in the Third World alive for a whole month. Embarrassing, isn't it?

FOOT IN MOUTH

A young couple had recently bought themselves a very old and shabby house and had spent ages doing it up and redecorating. They'd almost finished it and there was only one room to go when old friends called round for supper one night. The friends walked round the house admiring everything, then went into the dining room, where one wall was pale green and the other was a dark, murky grey. 'What a good idea to paint the walls light green,' said the friends. 'Such a pretty colour – it will look wonderful when it's finished.'

'Actually,' said the young husband, 'we're painting the room grey.'

READY WHEN YOU ARE, MR DE MILLE

This is a wonderful old story which has been told so often that no one can really remember whether it's true or not. But anyway, it's still worth hearing. In the 1930s and 40s one of the most famous of all film-makers was Cecil B. de Mille. He was best-known for his amazing religious epics, based on Bible stories and filmed against magnificent sets and scenery with no expense spared. During one of these films Mr de Mille was doing a spectacular and very difficult scene. When he gave the cue, hundreds of armour-clad actors had to run across the set, walls had to tumble to the ground, water had to flood in like a great tidal wave and horses had to rear in terror. They only had one chance to get it all right, because once the water had flooded and the walls had tumbled they wouldn't be able to do it again. All day Mr de Mille and his staff rehearsed it time and time again until they were sure they'd got everything right. The four cameras positioned round the set were checked once more. The actors prepared themselves. Mr de Mille raised his hand and gave the cue to start everything. The actors raced across the set, the horses reared, the walls tumbled, the water flooded – all as planned. When it was all over there was great relief around the set. Then Mr de Mille started to check that it had looked okay to his cameramen. 'Did you get that, Camera One?' he asked.

'Yes, I got it,' came the reply.

'How about you, Camera Two?'

'It looked great from here.'

'Camera Three?'

'Perfect – everything as planned.'

'Camera Four?'

'We're ready when you are, Mr de Mille . . .'

COMEDIAN FALL OUT

Is there nothing that EMMA THOMPSON can't do? She acts, sings and dances, she starred in *Tutti Frutti* and her own series *Thompson*, and she's recently made a film with Rowan Atkinson. But it's not any of those things she remembers as causing her most embarrassing moment. For a comedian the worst thing that can happen when you perform is that no one laughs. Emma recalled the time she appeared at a rally for the Campaign for Nuclear Disarmament: 'My most embarrassing moment? What about dying the ultimate comedians' death standing on Nelson's column in front of 60,000 CND supporters? Not being laughed at when you're attempting to be funny is that much worse when it's happening on a national monument in broad daylight in front of thousands of people who don't know you from a bar of plutonium. I wore a bag over my head for a week!'

CAT'S TALE

In 1978 there was a firemen's strike and so the army was called in to take over fire-fighting and emergencies. In January they received a call to an emergency in South London, where an old lady's cat had got stuck up a tree. They arrived in their special green fire engine and with great efficiency put a ladder up against the tree, climbed up and rescued the stranded cat. The old lady couldn't thank them enough. She gave them all a cup of tea and waved goodbye as the fire engine drove off – and ran over the cat. Very embarrassing . . .

THE FIRST KISS

A kiss stopped traffic for hours in Rio de Janeiro a few years ago. It happened when a young couple had to stop their car at a red traffic light. While they

waited for the lights to change they had a quick kiss. The lights went green but still they kissed, and kissed, and kissed, despite the other motorists hooting and shouting around them. Eventually the police arrived and tried to pull them apart – and found that the wire braces round their teeth had got caught together. A dentist had to be called before the embarrassed youngsters could be separated.

HAVEN'T I SEEN YOUR FACE SOMEWHERE BEFORE?

The *Edmonton Sun* newspaper reported the story of a schoolboy who put a vase over his head and found that it was stuck. As if that wasn't embarrassing enough, his mother had to rush him to hospital on a bus. And to make the poor lad's embarrassment complete, she actually put his school cap on top of the vase to make his appearance look a bit more normal . . .

THE WRONG HUSBAND

A couple of years ago a reader wrote to a women's magazine telling of an embarrassing incident that had happened to her. She'd been out shopping one Saturday morning and got back to find her husband fixing the car. He was lying on his side underneath it with his legs and bottom sticking out, so she gave him a playful pinch on the bum and went indoors – where she found her husband in the kitchen looking for a spanner. Their neighbour had come round to help mend the car and it was his bottom she'd pinched. Very embarrassed, she went out to apologise to him. But instead of taking it as a joke, the neighbour didn't come out from under the car. In fact he didn't move. She and her husband pulled him out and found that he was unconscious; when she'd pinched him he'd been so startled he'd hit his head on a bolt under the car and knocked himself out!

HANG IT ALL

THE GREAT SORPRENDO is a magician with a difference, as you'll know if you've ever seen him on television. But before he became a magician he was an actor – and a serious actor, except for one night . . . 'I did an entire act of *Julius Caesar* with a wire coat hanger dangling from my toga, completely baffled as to why the audience were in fits of laughter. I took it off for the rest of the play, but wore it for the curtain call at the end!'

ACTION, LIGHTS, CAMERA – LUNCH . . .

Another embarrassing moment from the film world. The director Michael Curtiz was organising a scene in which lots of people stood on a beach and watched a motor cruiser come into view and dock in a harbour. He had spent all morning putting the actors on the beach into their correct positions and waiting for the sun and the clouds to look right. It was midday by the time everything was ready and at last he gave the signal for the boat to come motoring into view, 'Launch!' he yelled. And all those carefully-positioned actors walked off the beach and went to have their lunch.

NO, PRIME MINISTER

There was an embarrassing moment for MRS THATCHER last year when she gave a television interview and got a bit carried away on the subject of the Channel Tunnel. It would give people their first opportunity to travel across the Channel without ships for 40 million years, said the Prime Minister. This sent historians running to their telephones to point out that she was wrong by more than 39 million years. According to the experts, as recently as 6,500 years ago it was possible to walk across a land bridge that stretched across the Channel. After that time the sea swept the 'bridge' away and Britain became an island.

And while we're on the subject of the Prime Minister, guess who said this in 1969: 'No woman in my time will be Prime Minister or Chancellor or Foreign Secretary – not the top jobs. Anyway, I wouldn't want to be Prime Minister; you have to give yourself 100 per cent.' The person in question was none other than Margaret Thatcher.

NO CAMELS ALLOWED

When cartoonist Gerald Scarfe made a programme for BBC2 about follies – weird and wonderful buildings, most of which cannot be lived in – he finished his film by showing a huge concrete camel that he had built near his Chichester home. Very weird and wonderful it was too; in fact so weird that the planning department of his local council almost had a fit. Having shown off his camel on national TV, Mr Scarfe must have been embarrassed to receive a letter from the planners telling him that the beast didn't have planning permission and that it would have to come down.

WATCHDOG?

A couple living in New York had been burgled so many times that they bought themselves a watch-dog. The husband trained the dog to bark whenever strangers came to the door and the wife taught it to hold a basket in its mouth. They arrived back from work one day to find that the house had been burgled yet again. This time there was a note on the kitchen table from the thieves, saying what a wonderful animal the guard-dog was – so useful, in fact, that they had stolen it.

BAD LUCK BIGGINS

Larger-than-life star CHRISTOPHER BIGGINS had an embarrassing moment during a pantomime. 'During one of my panto engagements I was doing the song sheet – getting children out of the audience to sing a song on stage. I talked to a rather pale, quiet child, then moved on to the child on my left when suddenly I heard the child on my right vomit all over the stage. When I consoled him he threw up again. I asked all the children to leave the stage and the two 'policemen' in the panto came on and cleared it all up. Yuck!'

DOCTOR'S ORDERS

In 1978 a new doctor took over a practice at Taunton in Somerset and went to see one of his new patients, a seventy-four-year-old woman who had spent the last forty years in bed. As far as he could see there was nothing wrong with her, so he traced what had happened. Apparently, forty years before she had had 'flu and the old doctor had told her to go to bed and stay there until he came back. He forgot to make a return visit, so the lady had stayed in bed. After a few weeks she decided that she preferred staying in bed to being up and about and so she told everyone the doctor had instructed her to stay there. For forty years she was waited on hand-and-foot by her mother and then another relative. Finally in 1978 the new doctor came along and discovered to everyone's embarrassment that she shouldn't have been in bed at all.

MOTOR MISTAKES

Every time there is a road accident in which a car is damaged, the owner has to fill in a form for the insurance company, explaining how the accident happened and whose fault it was. Some of these claim forms are very funny – and rather embarrassing for the people who fill them in! Here are a few examples:

'I was just driving down the road when a tree hit me.'

'I swerved towards a man at the side of the road but he ran to the right. Then I swerved to the right and he ran to the left. Then he tried to run out of the way but I still managed to hit him.'

'My car had to take a sharp turn owing to an invisible truck.'

'Coming home I drove into the wrong house and collided with a tree I haven't got.'

'I thought my window was down, but it was up – as I discovered when I put my head through.'

MISTAKEN IDENTITY

Newspapers are famous for getting things muddled up, but the editor of a Kansas newspaper must have been particularly embarrassed at this mistake: 'Instead of being arrested, as we stated, for kicking his wife down a flight of stairs and hurling a lighted kerosene lamp after her, the Reverend James P. Wellman died unmarried four years ago.' Whoops!

CARRY ON SINGING

If you're a fan of *All Creatures Great and Small* you'll know that actress LYNDA BELLINGHAM plays the long-suffering wife of vet James Herriot. And she's perhaps even more famous for her role of the mother in the adverts for Oxo cubes! Her most embarrassing moment came when she was working on a programme called *General Hospital*, playing a nurse . . . 'I was in *General Hospital* in 1972 when I heard that Sammy Davis Junior was recording in the next studio. I was desperate to sing with him, so I sneaked in dressed in my nurse's uniform! When they stopped for a tea break I went up to Sammy Davis and told him of my ambition and he turned round and said, "Who the hell are you – First Aid?" Anyway, he agreed to sing and Jack Parnell and his orchestra played for us. Halfway through the song a huge security man picked me up and carried me out of the studio! Everyone got to hear about my adventure and took the mickey out of me – but at least I did it!'

WHAT, NO TROUSERS?

This story is told by several people who commute into London each day from Surrey and all of them swear they know the man to whom it happened.

He'd been to a party one evening before Christmas and had had too much to eat and drink, with the result that on his way to Waterloo station to catch the train home he was sick all down his jacket and trousers. It just so happened that earlier in the day he'd collected another suit from the drycleaners, so when he boarded the train he locked himself in the loo and stripped off his messy suit. It was so disgusting that he couldn't bear to take it home, so he opened the loo window and threw it out. Then, having washed and tidied himself up, he ripped open the dry cleaner's plastic bag and found his suit jacket – and a woman's skirt. No trousers. Terribly embarrassing. The strange thing is, though a lot of people say they knew the man to whom this happened, not one of them remembers how he managed to get home without being arrested . . .

UFO-BIA

Northern Irish farmer Thomas Hutchinson hit the news in 1956 when he reported that he had actually caught a UFO – an Unidentified Flying Object from outer space. He described the UFO as having a saucer-shaped base and being bright red in colour with dark red stripes. Unfortunately it had started to spin when he grabbed it and when he put it down for a moment it took off and disappeared into the clouds. Local people were flummoxed. Mr Hutchinson was not the kind of person who made stories up and they were rather worried in case the alien craft came back again. Fortunately there was no need to worry, because it didn't take long for the RAF to identify the 'UFO' as one of their weather balloons which had come adrift. Mr Hutchinson's face must have been as red as the balloon.

TALENT-SPOTTING

Fred Astaire was one of the greatest tap-dancing stars ever to appear in Hollywood movies, but the first talent scout he auditioned for didn't appreciate his talent. Having watched Fred go through his paces he wrote, 'Can't act, can't sing, slightly bald. Can dance a little.' Bet he could have kicked himself later.

UGLY MOMENT

TV funny man RUSS ABBOT had an embarrassing moment on stage. 'It happened when I was in pantomime in 1980/81 playing Buttons in *Cinderella*. I was backstage, dressed for the Cooperman scene, when I heard the show relay the Ugly Sisters calling for Buttons. Realising I was in the wrong costume I put on a dressing-gown and dashed onto the stage. I did the whole scene with Cooperman's red cloak hanging down below the gown, which gave away the next scene.'

THE CASE OF THE POISONED MILK

The case of the poisoned milk caused some embarrassment at Hampstead police station not so long ago. A carton of milk had been taken to the police station one evening as evidence in a case of poisoning. The carton was labelled and placed on the desk of the officer who was in charge of the investigation. Next morning the day shift of policemen arrived and decided to have a cup of tea before starting work. They were having a nice cuppa when the duty officer popped his head round the door and asked what had happened to the carton of poisoned milk. You guessed it; they'd drunk the evidence.

MURRAY HURRIES TO RUSTIE'S RESCUE

RUSTIE LEE is well-known for her cookery features on TV-am – and it was while she was on camera that she had a very embarrassing experience. 'One morning while I was filming live in the kitchen for TV-am I was joined by disc jockey Pete Murray. I was merrily telling the viewers about how fresh and lovely mangoes were when I cut into the one I was using for my recipe and, with the camera in close, I discovered that it was rotten. The deeper I cut, the rottener it got, until Pete Murray actually reached out and threw it away!'

ROLL OUT THE RED, WHITE AND BLUE

SARAH GREENE's most embarrassing moment happened at an airport. 'Several years ago I was backpacking across America, and never quite got the hang of "packing my back" properly. On returning to Gatwick and waiting by the baggage carousel for my rucksack to appear, there, in amongst everyone else's luggage, were a pair of stripey red, white and blue knickers. Along with everybody watching I laughed when I saw them, until I realised they were mine! I retrieved my rucksack but left the knickers there still going round on the carousel!'

SAFE AS HOUSES

According to a report in a Rome newspaper a few years ago, robbers trying to break into an office to steal wages were foiled by an ordinary door. When they couldn't open it they fired a number of bullets at the lock, but still it wouldn't open. When police caught them in the act the robbers were dumbfounded with embarrassment. The door wasn't even locked. They'd been trying to pull it open. If they'd only *pushed* it would have opened easily . . .

GOING UP IN SMOKE

In 1947 in Hollywood a film director was making a western. He was very careful about getting the details right so when he wanted to shoot a scene in which Red Indians sent smoke signals, he called in some real Red Indians to advise on how to make the scene look right. When the movie had been completed the director thanked the Indians for their help. 'How did you learn about smoke signals?' he asked them.

'We learned how to do it by watching the movies,' said the Indians. Ouch!

TALL STORY

A Midlands builder who specialises in doing up old houses was having great difficulty in getting hold of the right sort of bricks for his work. The bricks had to be old so that they were the right colour and texture to match with the old places he was renovating. So when he heard that a nearby factory was going to blow up its old chimney, built in the 1800s, he immediately phoned them up and made an offer for the bricks. They accepted it and they even allowed the builder the honour of blowing up the chimney himself. When the dust had settled he and his men started the job of clearing up and stacking the bricks. The builder was feeling very pleased with himself when one of his men came running over holding some of the bricks. Every one of them was a slightly curved, tapered shape, made specially to create the circular chimney. Not a single one of them was straight enough to be used for house-building. The builder was, as you can imagine, red with embarrassment.

OVERHEARD

EastEnders fans will know AMERJIT DEU as Dr Singh. He told us that he's had several embarrassing moments because of the microphones he's had to wear while filming TV shows. 'I was doing *Playbus* once and had a body mike attached to me – a body mike is a small microphone they hide inside your shirt or elsewhere. Once these things are attached you have to undress to take them off, so you wear them all day, and it's very easy to forget about them. Anyway, I was wearing one during rehearsals and forgot I had it on. I was talking to another actor about the director and being a bit rude, talking about my girlfriend – the kind of things you want to keep private – when I remembered I was wearing the mike and that *everyone* was listening to me! I was very embarrassed. The other embarrassing thing about these mikes is that unless you keep taking them off and putting them back on again, they go everywhere with you – even into the loo!'

LOSING HER HEAD

Mary Queen of Scots would probably have been embarrassed about something that happened on 8 February 1587, if she'd been able to see it. Sadly, that was the day her head was chopped off. When the executioner had done his work he picked up the head and held it by the hair – at which the head dropped to the ground again leaving him holding a wig. Poor Mary was completely bald . . .

NOT SO STUPID

Albert Einstein's teacher must have been embarrassed to discover that his pupil grew up to be the greatest scientific mathematician the world has ever known. Einstein's Theory of Relativity revolutionised modern mathematics and won him the Nobel Prize. Not so bad for a boy whose teacher thought he was stupid and once told him, 'Einstein, you will never amount to much.'

FORGETFUL FRY

If you're a *Blackadder* fan you'll know STEPHEN FRY. Unfortunately when we contacted him he didn't have a funny story to tell us . . . But we'll let him explain. 'I remember when I was asked, some time ago, to contribute to a charity book. All I had to do was write down My Most Embarrassing Moment. I consented readily and then . . . would you believe it? I couldn't think of a *single* episode in my life which was amusing, appropriate or decent enough for publication. You can imagine my mortification, discomfiture and embarrassment, I'm sure. Blushes all round!!!'

CAUGHT NAPPING

A French burglar broke into a house in 1964 and raided the fridge. In it he found some of his favourite cheese and also a bottle of champagne, so he finished both off. This snack made him feel sleepy, so up he went to the spare bedroom for a snooze.

Was his face red when the police arrested him in bed the next morning? It must have been!

SMASHING TIME

MAGNUS MAGNUSSON, TV's *Mastermind* presenter, told of his most embarrassing moment in Robert Morley's *Book of Bricks*. In it Mr Magnusson tells of the time he was making a television programme about the Roman Fleet which had been garrisoned at Dover more than a thousand years ago. The archaeologists were very proud about a red slate that they had dug up. It had the initials C.B. on it, standing for *Classis Britannicus*, which in Latin means Roman Fleet. The archaeologists carefully handed him this precious historical find – and Mr Magnusson dropped it, smash, on the ground.

NORFOLK NO GO

As well as writing her own best-selling books and answering people's problems in her agony column, CLAIRE RAYNER appears on a whole variety of television and radio shows and in magazines. This is the story she told us about one of her embarrassing moments. 'I was about fourteen, the age at which it is difficult to admit that you have the same bodily functions as other people. Together with a crowd of other people of my own age and of both sexes, I was on a boat on the Norfolk Broads chugging along towards the end of a very agreeable day. But one engine broke down, so the speed of the boat was extremely slow. On each side of the bank there were bullrushes for several feet, so there was no way the boat could get to the side. And me – I was dying to go to the loo! I suspect a great many other people were in the same situation; I know several of my girlfriends were. I rather think the boys were too. But, as I say, we were fourteen and there was no way we were going to admit this fact.

And then I had a brilliant idea: I ''fell'' overboard. I came up covered with green slime but with my bladder, at last, empty, and was dragged ashore under the accusing jealous eyes of all my friends, and spent the rest of the journey in comfort. They, of course, had to queue for the loo when eventually we did arrive – but me? I was fine. I'd got over my embarrassment.'

ON THE THRONE

The famous orchestral conductor Sir Thomas Beecham returned to his hotel in Manchester one night in 1939 after conducting a concert with the Hallé orchestra. As he walked into the lobby he noticed a lady sitting by the lift and recognised her immediately. The only problem was that though he knew her face, he couldn't remember anything else about her.

'Good evening,' he said, unable to ignore her. 'Did you enjoy the concert?'

'Oh yes, I did,' she replied, and they talked for a few minutes about music and the weather and other little things while Sir Thomas struggled to try and remember her name or who she was. Just as he was about to leave he suddenly remembered that she had a brother so he asked,

'And tell me, how is your dear brother?'

'He is well, thank you, Sir Thomas,' replied the lady.

'And what is he up to at the moment?'

'Oh, he's still the King, you know . . .'

DAYLIGHT ROBBERY

A few years ago the *New York Times* reported the tale of an insurance agent who was on his way to work in the subway system – which is rather like the London underground system – when a short, smartly-dressed man bumped into him very hard on a platform and then walked away. The insurance agent felt in his jacket for his wallet and found that it was missing. He'd been robbed! Just a few yards away he spotted the little man getting into a train, so the insurance agent dashed over and just managed to grab him by the back of his jacket collar as the doors of the train closed. He dragged the man out of the train and a few feet along the platform, but then the material of the jacket ripped and the little man ran off yelling. Though he was still furious that he'd had his wallet stolen, the insurance agent felt quite pleased that he'd ruined the thief's jacket. Fuming, he got to the office and just a few minutes after he'd arrived the phone rang. It was his wife, phoning to tell him that he'd left his wallet behind at home . . .

EGG ON FACE

Comedy star and famous bird-watcher BILL ODDIE told us of a time he now looks back on with embarrassment. 'When I was a little lad I lived in Quinton. Near to my house was an area called the Leasowes. There was a golf course and lovely woodlands with a few ponds and a canal close by. Whenever I could I used to go off there to look for birds. Unfortunately I also used to do something else too. Something I really should not have done. I went collecting eggs. I was very careful not to disturb the nests, and I only ever took one egg, but I still shouldn't have done it. Nowadays collecting eggs is illegal and I think young people also realise, better than I did, that it can only harm the birds. When I think back to my own naughty deeds I am rather ashamed. I'm also rather glad that one day something happened which made me give up my wicked ways.

'One day I found a big nest on the ground in long grass under a hawthorn tree. In it were about a dozen large golden-coloured eggs. They had been laid by a pheasant. I didn't have a pheasant's egg in my small collection. So should I take one? Obviously I shouldn't have done, but I couldn't resist. Anyway, in this case, I didn't feel quite so guilty because it was obvious that the eggs had been abandoned. They were all stone cold and the nest was soaking wet. Maybe the parent birds had been shot (I'm afraid that happens to quite a lot of pheasants). I had a feeling these eggs had been lying there for a long time. Just *how* long, I soon found out.

'I took them back to my house and tried to "blow" them. This normally involves poking little holes in each end and blowing out the liquid white and yolk. However, I found I couldn't blow these eggs, because the insides had gone all gooey. What's more they *smelt* pretty terrible. The truth was, they'd gone bad. Really bad. Nevertheless, I still wanted a pheasant's egg in my collection. So I did a *really* stupid thing. Instead of blowing them . . . I sucked them. I spat out the horrible-tasting contents pretty quickly, but not quickly enough. I was sick for hours! Served me right. And that was the day I threw away my egg collection and became a bird-watcher instead!

'Of course the reason *you* must never take birds' eggs is *not* 'cos they might make you sick. Nor is it 'just' because it's now against the law. The real reason is that these days there just aren't as many lovely woodlands as when I was a boy, and many of our birds find it hard enough to find anywhere to build their nests, without having to put up with

people raiding and stealing their babies (which is, after all, what egg collecting is). Besides, watching beautiful living birds beats looking at a boring old egg collection *any* day!'

'ALLO, 'ALLO, 'ALLO

In 1979 Austrian police were embarrassed to admit they had locked a suspect, Andreas Mihavecz, in a cell and forgotten him – for an amazing eighteen days! When he was eventually found, Andreas was miraculously still alive. In fact his eighteen days without food and water was a record.

WHAT A SLIP UP

MICHAEL CASHMAN, who played Colin in *East-Enders*, says that so many embarrassing moments leap to mind . . .' But I particularly remember playing Dickie Winslow in the play *The Winslow Boy* at Alan Ayckbourn's Scarborough Theatre. I rushed on stage, supposed to have just arrived from Oxford. The audience roared with laughter. I looked down as the other actor giggled, to find I was wearing a pair of tattered bedroom slippers with my smart tail suit! I decided to ignore them and carried on defiantly. The horror returns every time I see those old, torn, checked bedroom slippers peering at me in the corners of my mind!'

HURRICANE . . . WHAT HURRICANE?

The most embarrassing moment of TV weatherman MICHAEL FISH's life was, we bet, that fateful October day in 1987 when he stood in front of the cameras and said, 'A woman rang in to say she'd heard there was a hurricane on the way. Well, don't worry. There isn't.' Just a few hours later southern England was hit by the worst winds for 284 years!

But Michael Fish hasn't been the only man to get the weather disastrously wrong. In 1964 the Director of Taiwan's Provincial Weather Bureau made a broadcast in which he said, 'Hurricane Gloria will not strike Taiwan.' The next day the hurricane hit the island with such force that 239 people were killed. The unfortunate weatherman was arrested and sent to court on charges of negligence.

And in 1979 the Saudi Arabian news service broadcast the following weather bulletin. 'We regret we are unable to give you the weather. We rely on weather reports from the airport, which is closed because of the weather. Whether we are able to give you the weather tomorrow depends on the weather.'

TOOTH ACHE

Singer, comedienne and impressionist FAITH BROWN had a terribly embarrassing moment on stage . . . 'I had just had a bridge of four teeth fitted and was on stage singing one day when all of a sudden it popped out. I managed to grab it and put

it down the front of my low-cut dress and just went on singing. When I came off stage. I rushed back to the dressing-room and couldn't find the teeth anywhere. All I was left with was four teeth marks on my chest! My husband found them an hour later, under the curtains on the stage. I was so embarrassed it was almost curtains for me!'

BOUNCING AROUND

At the end of the tragic opera *Tosca* the heroine, called Tosca, sings a last song and then throws herself off the wall of a castle to her death. This effect is obtained by the singer climbing the scenery at the back of the stage and jumping off onto a mattress a few feet below. On one occasion, in New York in 1960 to be precise, the backstage staff decided to play a practical joke on the singer playing Tosca. Instead of giving her a mattress to jump onto, they gave her a trampoline. On the night, not suspecting what was going on, she gave a magnificent performance, climbed onto the 'wall' and leapt off. It was reported later that she bounced up above the castle no fewer than fifteen times, sometimes yelling and screaming, sometimes laughing – and sometimes upside down. Everyone agreed that it was a wonderful moment, but not the great tragic ending they had come to expect. The poor singer who played Tosca was so embarrassed at what happened that she refused to sing again there and went to San Francisco instead.

FIGHTING TALK

BBC boxing commentator HARRY CARPENTER has, like most sports commentators, made his fair share of mistakes. One of the most embarrassing must have occurred in 1974 when he was reporting live on the fight between Muhammed Ali and George Foreman. In round eight Mr Carpenter announced confidently to the millions watching, 'That's it. There's no way Ali can win this one now . . .' The moment he said it Muhammed Ali knocked his opponent out for the count.

Another classic embarrassing moment occurred in 1938 when Lieutenant-Colonel Tommy Woodroffe was reporting on a football match. Thousands of radio listeners heard him say, 'If there's a goal now, I'll eat my hat.' There was and, true to his word, he did!

IT'S A DOG'S LIFE

ESTHER RANTZEN gets into all kinds of embarrassing scrapes on *That's Life*, but this particular one sticks in her memory . . . 'We consumer-tested some pellets called "Scent Off", which were designed to stop dogs digging up the lawn. Interestingly enough they seemed to be dog aphrodisiacs, or else we'd just invited the ten most over-sexed dogs in Britain to the *That's Life* studio to test them. The resulting chaos put our audience figures up to 22 million, but many of our poor pot plants never recovered!'

THE CASE OF THE BUNGLING BANK-ROBBER

One of the most embarrassing attempts to rob a bank happened a few years ago when a young man called Colin Rich decided that he was going to live up to his name by holding up a bank in Ontario, Canada. He decided to wear a stocking over his head to disguise his face but discovered, when he tried it, that it didn't disguise it much – so to be on the safe side on the day of the robbery he wore *three* stockings. They certainly hid his face – but they also made it impossible for him to see where he was going. When he finally found the door of the bank and walked in, he couldn't see the counter. And when he finally located that, he reached into his pocket to pull out his gun – and pulled out his glasses case instead. Realising that the robbery wasn't going to work he ran out of the bank and hid behind a car. The police found him there a few minutes later.

COOKERY AND WOOD WORK

VICTORIA WOOD is one of the funniest ladies on television. She told us of an embarrassing moment when she was a student . . . 'I remember trying to impress some chap with my healthy lifestyle and having to hide a huge bowl of tinned mince and tinned potatoes under the pillow when he arrived at the door of my bedsit. Not very healthy and *very* embarrassing.'

THIS IS AN UPSTICK!

We hope the thief who staged a raid in a Southampton supermarket in 1977 was suitably embarrassed about his bungle. He walked round the store loading a shopping trolley with goods, then joined the queue at one of the check-out desks. The girl totted up the cost of all his goods and the thief gave her a £10 note. Then, as she rang it up and the drawer of the till opened, he grabbed the cash in the till and ran off, leaving his shopping behind. What's so embarrassing about that? you may be asking. Well, there was only £4.37 in the till, and he ran off leaving the check-out girl still holding the £10 note. So if you do your sums, you'll see that far from robbing the supermarket, the raider actually *gave* them £5.63!

ACCIDENT PRONE

This story has been told by several people, all of whom swear it is true. It contains not one, but two embarrassing moments. About seventy years ago a young man fell in love with a wealthy young girl who lived in a lovely country house in Sussex. One weekend he went to stay there, determined to ask the girl to marry him. The room he was given was old and full of antique furniture, and on the floor was a beautiful Oriental carpet. After supper on the first night he went up to bed and fell asleep. But a couple of hours later he woke up feeling thirsty and, without bothering to switch on the light, felt about for the glass of water he'd left on the bedside table.

As he fumbled around in the dark he heard something fall over, but he was so sleepy that he didn't bother checking to see what it was. Next morning when he got up he found that he had tipped over a bottle of ink and that it had made a great black puddle in the middle of the valuable carpet. After that he lost his nerve and didn't dare ask the girl to marry him.

He left it a few months until, he hoped, everyone had forgotten about the ink. Then he went back to see the girl again, determined this time to ask for her hand in marriage. He was greeted by the girl's mother who left him in the drawing-room while she

went to fetch her daughter. The young man walked around nervously for a bit, then sat down on a furry cushion on the sofa – except that the second he'd sat down he knew it *wasn't* a furry cushion. It was in fact the mother's Pekinese dog, and it was dead! Without waiting to see the girl he loved, he ran straight out of the house and never, so it's said, came back again!

THAT'LL TEACH HER

TV presenter SUE ROBBIE remembers an embarrassing moment from the days when she was a teacher. 'I was teaching in a very forward-thinking English Department at a comprehensive school in Cheshire. For the fourth-year exam, instead of the usual comprehension test where they read a passage and answer questions, we decided to put on a short play which the students could later write about.

We teachers performed on a small, makeshift stage in the gym. I was the youngest teacher and played the part of the headstrong teenage daughter. At one point the teacher playing "Mum" and I had to have a furious row. We both threw ourselves into the parts with vigour; unfortunately in my case a bit too vigorously. As I bad-temperedly slumped into my chair the leg slipped off the edge of the stage and suddenly both I and the chair were transported – to land in an ungainly heap at the foot of the stage . . . AND in front of 280 hooting 15-year-olds! There is no dignity at a time like that.'

JUST LIKE THAT!

Do you remember the famous television comedian Tommy Cooper who died a few years ago? He was well-known for his magic tricks that always went wrong and were, therefore, very funny indeed.

He decided to become a comedian after a very embarrassing incident when he was seventeen. At that time he was working as an apprentice shipbuilder, but in his spare time he liked to do magic tricks and so when a concert was staged in the firm's canteen Tommy went along to show everyone his magic. However as soon as he walked out on the stage he forgot everything he had planned and stood there gulping like a goldfish. Surprisingly, the audience thought it was funny. They thought it was even funnier when every trick he tried went horribly wrong. For his big finale he did a trick with a milk bottle. 'I'm going to put this paper over the milk bottle. Then I'm going to turn the bottle upside down and take the paper away. The milk will stay in the bottle.'

The audience waited in suspense. As he took away the paper, milk cascaded all over the floor, leaving him gulping and gasping, unable to say another word. Shaking, he walked off the stage – only to hear the audience screaming with laughter and giving him a huge round of applause. From that embarrassing moment on Tommy Cooper knew that though he was never going to be a brilliant magician, he was already a great comedian.

ACCORDING TO MR GOLDWYN

Samuel Goldwyn was one of the greatest film producers of his time, known throughout the world for his wonderful movies. But he was almost equally well-known for the terrible verbal slips and mistakes he made. They became so famous and well-loved that in the end Mr Goldwyn wasn't too embarrassed about them any more. Here are just a few of his slips of the tongue that made everyone laugh at him:

A verbal contract isn't worth the paper it's written on.

In two words: im-possible.

All this criticism – it's like ducks off my back.

Anyone who goes to see a psychiatrist needs his head examined.

He also got things wrong in other ways. One prime example, that had people laughing for a long time, occurred when he boarded a cruise liner to take him from New York to England. As he stood on the deck of the ship, waving to his friends and family below, *he* yelled to them, *'Bon Voyage!'*

DON'T BE AN AS(PEL)

Londoners know STEVE JONES for his LBC radio show – but if you don't live in London you'll know him all the same, because he introduces *The Pyramid Game*. He told us, 'My most embarrassing moment was when I was approached by a "fan" in a restaurant by Loch Lomond in Scotland. "Are you who I think you are?" said this young lady of about 13.

'"Well, yes I am," replied yours truly, preening myself and waiting to sign an autograph. "See!" shouted the girl, turning to her mother, "I told you, it *is* Michael Aspel."'

CONNING A CONNERY

JASON CONNERY is a star in his own right – you'll probably remember him for his starring role in *Robin of Sherwood* a year or two ago. His father is also a famous actor; he's Sean Connery, best-known for playing James Bond. This father/son relationship led to a confusing moment for Jason . . .

'My most embarrassing moment was when I was auditioned by Maggie Carter (a casting director who was casting *Never Say Never Again*, a Bond film which starred my father). She asked me if I had ever seen the old James Bond – reminding me that he was the one with the Scottish accent. Then she asked if there was any connection between us as we had the same surname. I said, "Son" – she thought I had said "none". She then explained that Sean Connery had final approval of the casting of the film and she asked if I thought he might know my work!!! She did have the grace to be very embarrassed! Possibly it was her most embarrassing moment too!'

A LOAD OF RUBBISH

Red faces at Oxfordshire District Council in 1982, when Mr Ivan Kernahan asked them to send round the dustmen to take away a load of rubbish. The council very promptly sent a gang of men to Mr Kernahan's farm to take away the garbage. Unfortunately they walked straight past the pile of boxes and old furniture that Mr Kernahan wanted to dispose of and took away an engine and a gearbox that he'd just bought to put in his car.

THE RIGHT IMPRESSION

GARY WILMOT

The Duchess of York, Jimmy Cricket, Mrs Thatcher *and* Madonna in your living room? They could be if you follow Gary Wilmot's advice and make – THE RIGHT IMPRESSION!

KNIGHT BOOKS

ODYSSEUS II: THE JOURNEY THROUGH HELL

TONY ROBINSON AND RICHARD CURTIS

"Circe, how do we get home from here?" asked Odysseus, putting his boots on.

Circe gently kissed his forehead and said, "There's only one person who can tell you that – the prophet Tyresisus."

"But he's been dead for hundreds of years!"

"Exactly," said Circe, and unrolled a torn and faded map. "If you want to get home, you must visit the Land of the Dead."

It had taken ten long, bloody years for the Greeks to win the Trojan War and now, Odysseus, their victorious leader, wanted nothing more than to return home to his wife and son.

What he didn't know was that the journey ahead would take more than ten years – and the journey through Hell was only a beginning . . .

KNIGHT BOOKS